Advance praise for
Everyone Wants to Go to Heaven, But...

This is the strangest, funniest, and truthful-est book I've read in a long time. C. McNair Wilson is a brilliant combination of Shel Silverstein and C.S. Lewis (not the C.S. Lewis, but Claude Samuel Lewis, a really funny guy who works at McDonald's.) If this is a religious book then I want to be religious.
—**Mike Yaconelli,** Author, Co-Founder and Owner of Youth Specialties

It's time we Christians stop taking ourselves so seriously, and start putting things into perspective—an eternal one. Quirky and hilarious, C. McNair Wilson turns conventional Christian concepts upside down and inside out—to help us see our faith from new angles for laugh-out-loud fun!
—**Carmen Renee Berry,** Co-Author of the *New York Times* Bestseller, *girlfriends*

A book virtually impossible to describe! Simply stated: for the reader seeking an author who writes and sketches with charm, tenderness, clarity, wit, carefully concealed scholarship, outrageous originality and the sense of high purpose, McNair Wilson is your man.
—**Brennan Manning,** Author of *The Ragamuffin Gospel*

Hey, I thought prophets were supposed to be serious and a little boring! But McNair Wilson makes us laugh while zinging us with insights about religion, society, and life in general. Wilson is like Micah, the Old Testament prophet, but with a sense of humor. This book made me chuckle and even laugh out loud. Read this; you will like it.

—**Jim Wallis,** author of *Faith Works,* Editor of *Sojourners* (a really serious magazine), and *Convener of Call to Renewal.*

I've long been in awe of C. McNair Wilson's career as a humorist. With the publication of *Everyone Wants to Go to Heaven But...,* I am more convinced than ever that had he chosen to use his prodigious humorous gifts for good, there's no telling what he could have accomplished.

—**Robert Darden,** Senior Editor of *The Door* magazine and the author of 26 books, including *On the Eighth Day, God Laughed,* the only book in recent years nearly as funny (and as insightful) as McNair's.

Thanks, Mr. Wilson, for many chuckles, a few belly laughs, a book I couldn't put down, and some wonderful if painful insights. And many, for me, out-of-sight illustrations.
—**Ken Medema,** Songwriter and Singer

C. McNair Wilson's delight-filled book is the best kind of comedy writing: laughter evoking, thought provoking, and just plain fun!
—**David McFadzen,** Executive Producer and Co-Creator of *Home Improvement* with Tim Allen

I know that God is glad about this book.
—**SARK** Artist/Author of *Succulent Wild Woman* and *Transformation Soup*

Also by C. McNair Wilson

Books
YHWH Is Not a Radio Station in Minneapolis
Illustrations for Other People's Books
Freeze-Dried Songbook (Sonny Salsbury and Tim Hansel)
Good Advice (Jim Hancock and Todd Temple)
Plays
The Fifth Gospel
From Up Here
Raised in Captivity
A Christmas Carol (from Charles Dickens)
Musicals
Love You Spoke a Word (Songs by Ken Medema)
How the West Was Saved (Songs by Sonny Salsbury)
Videos
Imaginuity: Recapturing Your Creative Spirit
Websites
www.mcnairwilson.com

Everyone Wants to Go to Heaven, But . . .

Gary—

The sky is NOT the limit!

C. M. Mair Wilson

Welcome to
EDEN
Beware of Snake

Everyone Wants to Go to Heaven, But . . .

Written, Illustrated, and Refereed by

C. McNair Wilson

PageMill Press
Berkeley, California

EVERYONE WANTS TO GO TO HEAVEN, BUT...
WIT, FAITH, AND A LIGHT LUNCH

Copyright © 2000 by Craig McNair Wilson
Cover illustration by C. McNair Wilson
Author photo by Patrick House, Pasadena, California

Publisher: Tamara Traeder
Editorial Director: Roy M. Carlisle
Marketing Director: Carol Brown
Managing Editor: Leyza Yardley
Proofreader: Shirley Coe
Production Coordinator: Larissa Berry
Typesetting: Larissa Berry
Cover Design: ID Graphics
Interior Illustrations and Calligraphy: C. McNair Wilson

Typographic Specifications: Body text set in Lo-Type Light 11.5/16; Headers, throughout, various fonts, many are hand-drawn by C. McNair Wilson

Printed in Canada.

Library of Congress Cataloging-in-Publication Data
Wilson, C. McNair.
    Everyone wants to go to heaven, but– : faith, wit, and a light lunch /
    written, illustrated, and refereed by C. McNair Wilson.
        p. cm.
    ISBN 1-879290-16-2 (alk. paper)
        1. Christian life–Humor. 2. Bible–Humor. I. Title.
    BV4517 .W556 2000
    230'.002'07–dc21

                                                    00-043446

PageMill Press, 2716 Ninth Street, Berkeley, California 94710.

10 9 8 7 6 5 4 3 2 1   00 01 02 03 04

Dedication

For
Mae,
Slev,
Sonny,
Kraning,
Ben,
Wayne and Mike,
Denny,
Buchfuehrer,
Dick,
and
Jack Green,
who let me laugh
about my faith
first,
loudest,
and most.

Contents

Foreword

Every once in a while someone comes along who rattles your cage. I don't mean they just shake it a little. They tip it over and break open the lock and invite you to taste of freedom. That is what Craig McNair Wilson does. He is a professional cage rattler. He did it when he worked in Imagineering at Disney and as a result they created better parks. He did it every time we worked together. When C. McNair Wilson is in front of an audience he changes lives. You can hear cages tipping over and people screaming with the joy of being free.

When *Everyone Wants to Go to Heaven, But . . .* came in the mail I opened it to a cartoon on "quiet times and homeless people" and laughed till I was sick. He had instantly dragged me back thiry-five years and exposed an old religious myth for what it was. A myth! In the midst of laughter I was released from whatever tenuous hold the old myth might still have had on me. That's the thing about McNair. He's not just funny. He is intelligently, honestly, and dangerously funny.

I skipped around in the book like a kid digging through a toy box. Finally, I sat down and read it from cover to cover. It sat on our coffee table for three weeks and I kept going back to it like some kind of junkie. Last week someone stole it.

Bottom line? I love this book. Whoever has it now, loves this book. It's like an Oreo cookie. You can eat the front first, the middle first or the back first. But wherever you start you will eat the whole thing. Only McNair can nestle such delightful, and sometimes pro- found filling between layers of delicious lunacy. When they come to take him away, I want to go with him. Enjoy!

Ken Davis
Author, Humorist, Professional Wrestler

Everyone wants to go to

but no one wants
to buy a ticket.

Preface

Forty Years in the Making

For the longest time, I felt out of place in the family of God. Truth to tell, I've been scribbling, doodling, noodling, and performing this material most of my life—to the great consternation of Sunday school teachers and other ecclesiastical overseers.

Oh, there was humor in church. Virtually every sermon I heard growing up started with a joke. Not one of these jokes had even the mose remote connection to the lesson du jour. There was also laughter at church social gatherings, and there were summer camp skits. All this yucking it up by church folk was disconnected from the pursuit of faith.

In the early 1960s a handful of youth speakers started telling comic versions of David and Goliath and other overly familiar Bible tales. Meanwhile, I was getting into trouble for my satirical takes on preachers, prophets, and the relentlessly pious.

Enter Bill Cosby, *The Tonight Show* with Johnny Carson, 1964. The piece was "Noah!" At last there was an opening, a kindred spirit. Then in high school, my father gave me a book of contemporary parables written by a friend of his. The friend was Joe Bayly, the book was *I Saw Gooley Fly* (Fleming H. Revell, 1968, later republished as *How Silently, How Silently* by David C. Cook. It was amusing, even silly, but always riveting storytelling and with a message—an eternal objective. About that same time my creative writing teacher at a church-related high school gave me Thomas Howard's *Christ the Tiger* (J. B. Lippincott, 1967.) In the first paragraph, he describes his childhood in a church family as "a massive effort to get cozy." I felt like Tom Howard had been following me around. I wasn't alone. I also discovered the Quaker theologian Elton Trueblood's look at the comedy of the Old and New Testaments in his book *The Humor of Christ* (Harper & Row, 1964)—still an important work. Somebody else out there—three somebody else's— were using humor to navigate their journey of faith. Trueblood introduced me to a broader, fuller image of Jesus. *Christ the Tiger* freed me to be myself and embrace that image, while *Gooley* would be the nonesuch for a style of writing and storytelling to which I wanted to aspire. All three were the beginning of a long journey away from the numbing nonsense of the church's restrictive legalism that served as an incessant "shhhh" to my wit and wondering.

In the early 1970s I began to question the institutional side of faith. I had not stopped believing in God or the efficacy of the cross of Christ. I began to tell and act out stories that dealt with the human side of Jesus for friends. When I shared a handful of these stories with a pastor friend (Ben Patterson), who had been a mentor in my quest for a faith beyond simple Sunday school stock answers to inner life, he invited me to assemble them into an evening of what was to have been a one-night only "performance." Following that three-hour improvisation for the high school and college folk at our church, I was invited to present my new "play" to other campus ministry groups in our area. In my play I wondered aloud about Jesus and the disciples having a water and mud fight on a hot day, or mixing saliva and dirt to make mud to put in a blind man's eye to restore his sight, or hiding behind a bush to sneak a peek at the most beautiful girl in town. The assembled group of eighty friends roared that first night. Thus was created my first one-man play, *The Fifth*

Gospel, in January 1972. (It has since been performed more than 1,500 times, along with another one-man play, *From Up Here.*) After more than five hundred performances of that one-man play, I discovered what was to be one of the most important books in my journey.

The door to my imagination—in the context of faith—was kicked open and off of its hinges when I first read Madeleine L'Engle's *Walking on Water* (Harold Shaw, 1980). I was no longer uncertain of the propriety of my musings about faith. As a result of my conjecturing aloud about Jesus as a normal male adolescent—girlfriends and all—and my ravings in the pages of *The Door* magazine, I began to have second, third, and twelfth thoughts about the value of my religious humor. Many in the church flat out criticized my use of theater arts. Madeleine helped me see that what I was up to was art, and it was humor, and it was okay. Just as sure as it was okay for Jesus, the man, to walk on water. Madeleine wrote, "God is constantly creating, in us, through us, with us, and to co-create with God is our human calling." It seems to be the conspicuous calling of the artist, especially the artist who is also Christian.

I continue to disturb ardent believers with my plays, writing, and cartoons, hoping to shake some of the dust off of their comfortably beigianity. To those who do not yet have a personal faith in the Creator, I hope they will find in my work, especially in these pages, a response to some of their questions, even the oft-repeated cliché queries.

Consider, please, the wacky notion that our Creator may be as much fun as we can be. Maybe God finds our foibles, selfishness, and religiosity even more amusing than we do. What if God came to Earth and lived among us? What if it has already happened?

Along my way I was encouraged by my recurring association with *The (Wittenburg) Door* magazine, where I published many of my articles and cartoons that form the early sketches that have become this book and my first book, *YHWH Is Not a Radio Station in Minneapolis* (HarperSanFrancisco, 1983). Much of that (out-of-print) book is folded into these pages.

A book that took forty years to write? This is it. *Heaven . . . But* is arranged alphabetically, "but" you can jump in anywhere. Read it aloud to a friend. Let me know where it takes you. It took me most of my life to create.

If you haven't spent much time in the Bible, you will still enjoy this book. If you don't own a Bible, stop by any Protestant or Catholic church, and they'll give you one. If they won't, just come back on Sunday morning and help yourself to one of the Bibles they keep in the pew racks. Be sure to put a few bucks in the offering plate when it comes by and tell 'em McNair sent you.

C. McNair Wilson
Rockridge Cafe, window seat,
English Breakfast tea, with milk and honey

Acknowledgments

Who Are All Those People on the Dedication Page?

All my life there has been laughter and always there has been God. Putting the two together has not always been accepted. Early on and before it was permissible, let alone popular, there were a few who let me be funny about my faith. Some even encouraged me with cash.

Chief among them are the friends to whom this book is dedicated (see page ix). There were others, but these ten were the most vociferous, the most vivid.

The last name on the dedication list was the first to embrace and celebrate my warped way of experiencing my faith. Jack Green was my seventh grade homeroom teacher at San Gabriel Christian School and the best teacher I have ever known. Every encounter with Mr. Green, whether teaching history, Spanish, or Bible was an occasion for magnificent discovery. Most importantly he found ways to make me want to complete my class work "quickly, so we can get to work on that bulletin board." He showed me how to be creative in all areas of my life—as he was with his life.

My mother's best friend was the coordinator for the high school group in our church. Mae Fitzgerald thought everybody and everything was "neat." Mostly she was right. She found giftedness in each of us and encouraged and affirmed our individuality. I'm sure she did not always appreciate my unsolicited running commentary in Sunday school, but she never put me down for my humor. She was the first person to pay me for my art—$5 to create a car wash/fundraiser poster. She also let me perform my ventriloquism and magic for church social activities, not just for my peers, but for college and adult groups, as well as at other churches. This all began when I was ten years old—I came under Mae's aegis long before I was in high school.

I was also invited to be on the summer staff at Forest Home Christian Conference Center earlier than the age requirement, which was eighteen. I was sixteen when Jim Slevcove created a place—several places—for me to be myself on staff at Forest Home. Slev was, and is, a wise mentor, friend, and frequent audience. I've always delighted in making Slev laugh.

At Forest Home I made several lifelong friends and encouragers for my harebrained homilies.

When Sonny Salsbury was "on the hill" making music as a composer and song leader, Forest Home was a better place. Later Sonny and I would collaborate in creating stage musicals and an illustrated songbook. Sonny is one of those creativity-from-every-pore-of-his-body people. His faith is expressed the same way. Meanwhile, in another part of the Forest (Home), Bob Kraning stood in front of a roaring fire every week, six nights a week, and told my junior high friends and me about God. Bob is a powerful communicator and always hilarious. Unlike too many youth speakers, Kraning's humor grew out of stories from the Bible. They were not pasted-on jokes attempting to spice up dead, overused Bible tales. In subsequent summers Kraning was an early mentor in the art of justifiable jocularity and the power of humor. We were always making each other laugh, frequently about the stuff of faith. Forest Home was also where I met the first person who made me think about my faith—Ben Patterson. He introduced me to the writings of theologians whose books are not on the front tables at your local Christian bookshop—if they are even there at all. Ben was, and is, a compelling Bible teacher who is at once a student of history, current events, and the eternal heart of the Creator.

As a junior high camper at Forest Home's Lost Creek Ranch, I encountered two characters that I still can't shake loose. The Ranch was run by the indefatigable Wayne Rice and the ever-dangerous Mike Yaconelli. With the addicts running the pharmacy, every night was skit night at the Ranch. They let me do my ventriloquism, magic, mime—everything and anything. There seemed to be no end to the silliness when Wayne and Mike were around.

That continued when in 1971 (through Ben Patterson) they invited me to become art director, film critic, cartoonist-in-residence, and resident young 'un at their fledgling magazine, *The (Wittenburg) Door.* Along with my wit, they let me express my consternation with the church for its many sillinesses. (I continue to contribute to *The Door* all these decades later.) Whenever I'm with Wayne or "Yac" there is lots of laughter—and no small amount of mischief. On a slow day it's only mischief.

At *The Door* I connected with Denny Rydberg, the editor. Though I was merely nineteen when hired, he made me an equal, considering my opinions at staff round tables and employing many of my edgy ideas in the pages and on the covers of the magazine. I had virtual artistic freedom (as long as I was in my office by 9 A.M. I changed *that!*)

During my high school years, I bumped into Jim Buchfuehrer (pronounced "Collins"). Jim, Campus Life Director (San Jose,

California), gave me free reign in his large campus ministry—to assist him both in programming and staff training. Like Ben Patterson, "Boof" was interested in the deeper issues of faith and always with laughter. Boof introduced me to Dick Sherman, a local youth pastor and a rare renaissance rabbi. Thoughtful, theatrical, playful, and warm—like a bonfire—Dick forever changed my view of faith lived institutionally. This was the 1960s in the San Francisco Bay area. Dick encouraged every person that strolled through his youth groups (junior high through college) to fully explore the passions given to us by the Creator.

In the here and now, I am buoyed by four remarkable, close friends who continue the redemptive acts that began with Jack Green more than forty years ago. Max Miller, my business partner for nearly two decades, has been a compass to both hemispheres of my brain. He is, quite simply, one of the more insightful and silliest creatures in the civilized world and would fit quite comfortably in most uncivilized worlds. Max constantly encourages me and holds me accountable. Stoking the fires that Max so often holds my feet to is my dear friend Susan Kennedy (a.k.a. SARK)—an enormous spirit. She deservers a separate book to cover the tenacious encouragement and sturdy love that she has brought to my life. In public and in private Susan quickens my resolve to be more fully expressed. Together we discovered that "bigger than life" can be actual size. I am less fearful of being me because of Susan and Max.

There are thousands of speakers in the family of God who teach the Gospel and many who use humor, but none combines the two as hilariously and seamlessly as my friend KenDavis.com. For more than a decade he has relentlessly and unflinchingly encouraged both my personal and professional growth. He pushes me toward excellence—often beyond what I imagine possible. Much of this book's existence is Ken's fault.

The fourth friend is Roy M. Carlisle—who, as it happens, is also editorial director for this publishing company. He makes my words better. He never lets me get away with mere quips, except over Sunday brunch at the Montclair Egg Shop. (You can join us after 1 P.M. most Sundays.)

None of this would have ever occurred—even as doodles in my (more than one hundred) sketchbooks—had it not been for my mother and father who taught me to trust God and ask everyone else lots of questions.

Blessings, too, to the entire Ninth Street gang (Wildcat Canyon Press staff) for their keen and steady commitment to fashioning excellent books both in content and design. Special kudos to the unflagging efforts of Larissa Berry who wove hundreds of pieces of art and verbiage into one book. Special accolades (and Rolaids) to Wildcat cochief, Tamara "Mergers-R-Us" Traeder, for taking on my book even though we are also friends.

Writing is a solitary practice. Living is done on a busier stage. From Adam's first breath, the Creator knew that "it is not good that (humankind) be alone." For me there have been hundreds of folks along the road whose laughter, comments, and feedback have been valuable. The trick is paying attention and sorting through the din to discern the good stuff. The stuff that really works in our life. The stuff that is true. Thanks to all. Now go to your rooms and leave me alone for a bit.

Adam

FIRST PERSON, FIRST LETTER. Adam was the first person to do just about everything: eat, talk, climb trees, and fall in love. (*See* Eve.) Adam was not, however, the first person to use a Veg-O-Matic. Adam was not unemployed. He was given a very important job. It was, in fact, the first job anyone had ever been given. God asked Adam to give everything a name. (Before Adam came along, God just pointed and said, "This thing here," or "That thing over there." And sometimes God would say, "No, not that one—the other one." And that's where all those sayings came from.)

So Adam sat on a rock all day, and when he saw something that he had never seen before, he would say, "This is a duck, that is a bush, this a Weimaraner, and you are a sandwich!"

After several hours of naming things, Adam turned to someone near him and said, "Look, be an angel and get me something to drink."

And that's how angels where named.

Anger

[Of pigeons and postcards]

ANGER CAN BE A HELPFUL EMOTION: a release, a catharsis, and it can ease tension built up for too long. A good scream can clear the mind just as a good scrubbing cleanses caked-on dirt from beneath hard-laboring fingernails.

Anger can also be an effective means of communication.

When Jesus stormed into the Temple and got angry with the money changers and sacrificial animal salesmen, he did more than free sheep, unburden birds, and rearrange the furniture in the temple courtyard. With feathers, postcards, and cassette tapes flying everywhere, Jesus was trying to teach us something: "Don't turn God's house into a supermarket." He didn't want the lobby of a house of worship to become a roadside souvenir stand along the highway to Heaven.

If Jesus were appearing at your church, I do not think he would sell you a picture of himself for a dollar. There would be a small sign on his table that read, "We are out of graven images, ask the band at the next table."

ARK

IT WASN'T NOAH'S ARK, it was God's ark. Noah was the general contractor. The ark took one hundred and twenty years to build because it was huge. No one had ever had a backyard project quite this big before. Not surprisingly, Noah and his sons made a few mistakes along the way. He couldn't just turn on public television and get ideas from Boaz Villa on "This Old Ark."

To make room for the construction site, Noah had to get easements from several of his neighbors. Some took to calling Noah's harebrained project the "Gopher Goose."

"It'll never float!" they taunted Noah constantly.

"Why, heck, there's no water for cubits around."

There was also no marine supply store so Noah and his guys had to make everything themselves. They even had to make their own rope. Eventually they learned the ropes, and how to hang a waterproof door. Everyone pitched in.

The pungent fragrance of tar would not soon leave the ark.

I always wondered whether there was a pair of woodpeckers on the ark, and if so, did they have muzzles on their beaks? Or, perhaps, duck tape?

There's always more to life than we can prepare for—more, too, than we can imagine. Often, there's more than we can handle. Even the smartest among us ask for help.

As a child of the '50s I grew up watching years of TV. The invincible Roy Rogers, whenever he was in a jam, or in a box canyon being held down by the bad guys, would slap his trusty horse, Trigger, on the rump and say, "Go get help!"

Noah finished God's ark with help from three sons, several grandsons, scores of great-grandsons and great-great-grandsons.

Along the way he asked the client lots of questions.

Atheist

I TRIED BEING AN ATHEIST, but they don't have enough holidays. Come to think of it, they don't have any holidays. It is a belief system that exists not to believe in something. If there really is no God, why do we need atheists to tell us that?

We have no anti-blue elephant group?

Authorized Version

IT'S NOT THE KING JAMES VERSION of the Bible, printed in the year of our Lord 1611, but the unofficial assumptions of church life that have become part and parcel of our beliefs. Can you find what is false, if anything, in the following statements?

- The world was created in six days of twenty-four hours each.
- The forbidden fruit that Adam and Eve ate was an apple.
- Jonah was swallowed by a whale.
- Baby Jesus was visited by three kings (wisemen and astrologers) in his stable/birthplace in Bethlehem.
- Jesus told us to "eat, drink, and be merry."
- Neither a borrower nor a lender be.
- At the wedding feast at Cana, Jesus' first miracle was turning water into grape juice. ("Wine" was the word they used when they meant fruit juice. As in Proverbs, when wise old King Solomon suggested giving "strong fruit juice to a man that he might forget his troubles.")

BABEL

BABEL OR "BABBLE." In the Old Testament, Babel was a bunch of people who thought they could reach God by touching the sky. But God didn't like their idea, so he confused them. And they didn't understand each other, and they didn't get any work done, and they didn't reach God. (*See* Nimrod.)

Today a lot of people still babble. Some are understood, and some are not.

BAD NEWS

THE BAD NEWS IS THAT YOU BLEW IT and you're in big trouble—it's going to cost you. The good news is that Jesus paid your "bill" even before you said you were sorry for screwing up.

The bad news is that you won't admit that you messed up.

The good news is that they have now figured out that it was probably somebody else's fault, no matter what it was you did. Relax. You didn't do nothin'.

The bad news is that now you're in trouble for doing nothing.

Baloney

NAZARETH

BALONEY

Estate Grown
V I N T A G E
39 AD.

Grown, processed, Bottled
NAZARETH BALONEY CO. Ltd

(Keep Refrigerated)

NOT EVERYONE BELIEVES IN GOD. Whether you believe in God or not, you have reasons for your belief—or absence of belief. Sometimes these reasons are excuses for not taking a good look at the possibility of God. Lots of people don't believe because God doesn't seem to be what they want God to be. Maybe they expect God to end all human suffering with the wave of a magic wand or the snap of God's super-powerful fingers. (*See* Pain and Suffering.) On the other hand (the non-snapping fingers hand), those who believe in God don't all believe for exactly the same reasons. They tend to pick and choose what parts of God to believe in, teach, and emphasize in their lives.

One example of this is the very first miracle Jesus ever performed—turning water into wine. The wine Jesus made from water at the wedding (after they ran out of the good stuff) wasn't really wine at all. Actually, it was grape juice! Everybody knows that when the wedding feast was finally over, they took all the leftover grape juice and put it back into the refrigerator so it would not turn into wine.

Jesus could not possibly have made wine. Wine is bad. Wine makes you goofy and drunk. That's bad. Jesus would never do anything to cause people to act goofy. So Jesus would never have made real wine. That's goofy.

Please pass the baloney.

BUS DRIVER

WALLY PEAT, CHURCH BUS DRIVER for First Church downtown, was fired last Monday for yelling at Melody Naramore and making her cry. It seems that Melody had her head out the window—

again—and was *spitting* into the open, driver's-side windows of passing autos. Though the church agreed with Wally that Melody's behavior was inappropriate and dangerous, they did not concur with Mr. Peat's chosen method of discipline.

He stopped the bus, walked back to where Melody was expectorating, and shouted, "Sit down, you little fart!"

An announcement was placed in the church bulletin the following Sunday: "Until a permanent replacement can be hired, the church bus will be driven by associate pastor, Ed Holt, beginning this Sunday. Melody has had her bus privileges rescinded for thirty days, pending a thorough review by the Committee on Church Bus Behavior and Maintenance."

CAIN

THIRD LETTER AND THIRD PERSON. Cain was the first son of Adam and Eve. But he was not the number one son. One day it was time for everyone to bring in their homework. Cain did the assignment wrong. Abel, his brother, did it right. God gave Abel an A. Cain got an F.

When you're No. 2, you try harder. Sometimes you try too hard. So . . . Cain killed Abel.

CAMEL

A RICH MAN TOLD JESUS, "Look, I have all this stuff: a beach house, a mountain cabin, cars, clothes, wine cellar, yacht, and a factory-direct furniture warehouse."

This guy was really shekels-up.

Then he asked Jesus, "Do you think I can get into Heaven?"

His question seemed simple enough. Jesus' answer wasn't.

"Ha!" Jesus laughed. "It would be easier for a camel to squeeze through a keyhole than for a rich man to get into Heaven."

Ever since then, preachers, rich people, and especially rich preachers have argued about what Jesus meant by this lesson. What do you think?

A. Rich people can't go to Heaven.

B. Camels can't go to Heaven.

C. Rich camels can't go to Heaven.

D. All keyholes in Heaven are small.

CENTURION

POLICE. Roman police to be specific. In the days of Jesus, they were pretty much in charge of the whole world (as far as they could tell at the time). Today the police in Rome direct traffic. Rome has some of the best traffic jams in the world. The Roman police force has gone downhill in the last two thousand years.

Children

WHO WE USED TO BE and wish we still are.

To get into some movies, a child needs an adult guardian. To get into Heaven, all adults will need a child's heart. Or a child to vouch for them.

Bring two, just in case.

Chronicles

IN THE BIBLE THERE ARE TWO BOOKS called "Chronicles."
In San Francisco, California, they have a brand new *Chronicle* every
day. God has a lot more to say to San Francisco.

Cleaver

WHEN I WAS A LITTLE KID, watching television one night, I asked my dad, "Will the Beaver be in Heaven?"

My dad said, "Leave it to Jesus."

I guess father knows best.

CREATION

GOD ROLLED MUD AROUND IN HIS HANDS and created human life. (*See* Mud.) Does God have hands? How many hands? How many fingers? How many fingers is God holding up? Why is God holding up his fingers?

Wait, is he pointing at something? At me? No, I think God is pointing at you. What's that, God? Are you pointing at me? Are you sure you don't want to be pointing at someone else?

CREATION 2
The First Monday After Creation

THEY HAD RESTED FOR A WHOLE DAY—twenty-four hours. It was the very first day off ever. They had more than earned it. Six days straight of work, work, work, with very little sleep and remarkably short lunch breaks. (Along with heaven and earth, they had also created the lunch break.) All that was behind them now. Then, all of a sudden, where there had never been a "there" there, there was Creation. They also created "there." ["They" are all God's helpers. In the Book of Genesis, God said, "Let us make human beings in our image." Jesus helped too. When he came to Earth Jesus continued to help around his father's shop.]

Now it all started, on this first Monday after Creation: buses filling up with commuters on their way to their first job interview, and the first cup of morning coffee to be brewed, forgotten and become bitter, thrown out and a fresh pot made for the lunch crowd. It would be the first lunch crowd ever. And in the first load of laundry ever washed, the very first sock would be lost. (*See* Shepherd.)

A farmer would milk his first cow and later, in town, a little boy would drink his first big, cold glass of milk—leaving a big, white mustache on his upper lip. As he ran off to catch the first bus to his first day of school, ever, his mother would shout to him to *wipe the milk off your upper lip.* She would do that on many more mornings. He was in a hurry, for on top of everything else, this was the first day of the first game of the first team of the very first season of softball.

Now that the milk mustache had been wiped from his lip, he could throw out the first pitch. The world has not been the same since.

But what about the last pitch? The last catch? The last out in the last inning of the final game? We can all remember the great firsts of our lives: first bike, first date, first taste of sushi, first pierced earrings, first airplane flight, first romantic kiss, first motorcycle ride, first mountain hike, first part in a play. Opening night!

What about the *lasts*? The final times. Things you would never do again. Did you know at the time that it would be the very last time? Would you have done it differently if you had known that it was absolutely the last time? Would you have done it better? Would you have done it at all? If you knew that you would never do it again . . .

cri'ttics

IT SEEMS AS THOUGH more and more often these days, there are a lot of people, especially in the media, picking on church folk. The press and Hollywood appear to be watching churches closely and pointing out and picking on every little mistake we make.

Maybe they learned this annoying practice from us church folk.

SOME WALK, some stroll, some shuffle, some skip, some jog, some race, some dance.

Children, artists, and angels dance.

Dance. It's the way God gets from place to place.

It's the way your body says, "I hear the music!"

DEATH IS A DOOR with two sides. One side says "Exit" and the other side says "Enter."

WHAT IF THE CHURCH were more like an old roadside diner?

Open twenty-four hours a day, seven days a week. "We never close. We serve anyone." The coffee is always hot, and all the cups are bottomless. Every waitress knows you, and they've had the same chef for years.

The linoleum floor has been walked on so much, it shines. In the bright morning light of the sun it almost looks like . . . well, you'll see.

Next time you're in downtown St. Paul, Minnesota, walk over to Mickey's Diner and have breakfast—anytime. You'll see. It's a little slice of Heaven.

Donkey

THE FIRST TIME THEY TRANSLATED THE BIBLE into
English—around the time of Shakespeare—they called a donkey an
"ass". Today the word ass is used to imply not a donkey, but . . .
someone's, ah . . . duff. As in, "get off your duff and get to work."
Ass is a bad word and we should never call a person an ass.

These days in Sunday school they teach kids the "Story of
Balaam's Duff."

In the Old Testament we learn about the time when God used
the Balaam's ass to speak to him in a flash of light. Even today, once
in a while, following an old biblical tradition, God still speaks
through an ass.

IT'S NOT THE ENEMY OF FAITH. Doubt is the honest, rigorous inquiry after truth. The enemy of faith is not caring.

END of the World

Epistle,

THE BIBLE IS FULL OF LETTERS and letter writers. The most famous and prolific letter writer was the Apostle Paul. He wrote letters and sent them all over the "known world." (That's what they used to call Asia Minor, which is now known as the Middle East.)

Most of Paul's letters were sent to famous churches in Ephesus, Galatia, Second Corinth, and other places. Paul never wrote to anyone in Dallas.

Paul wrote to all these churches because they were messed up, confused, and constantly arguing about almost everything. If the first-century church had been in better shape, the New Testament would have been much shorter. And Paul could have stayed home more and had a girlfriend.

Instead he wrote lots of letters and traveled to all of the places he wrote to.

His most famous letter was written to the Italian Christians. In those days, most Italians lived in and around Rome (the capital city and the place where the main post office was). So Paul's letter to Italy was called, "Letter to All Christians in and Around Rome and Their Friends."

To this day a lot of Italians still live in Rome. They are called Romans. A lot of Italians do not live in Rome. They are just called Italians.

It's kind of like people who are Christians. Some go to church and some do not. The ones who go to church are called Christians. The ones who don't go are called *absent.*

Someday all Christians will be together in Heaven with God. Except those who are absent.

Eternal Life

THE LONGEST DAY of your life. (See pages 64 and 65.)

EVANGELISM

IT IS NOT SOMETHING YOU DO; it is something you are. It's something you feel, not something you hear. It is what true believers do, all the time, by just living their lives every day—except when they are napping or in a coma.

Evangelism is not noisy, but it is very loud.

EVE

THE FIRST LADY. Eve was the only lady for a while. When you are the first lady—like the president's wife—you have to be careful about what you say, how you behave, and what you wear in public. Back when Eve was in public there was never any public there to watch her, so she . . .

EVIL

EVIL IS MURDER AND GREED and selfishness and Larry swiping your new bike and hiding it in the bushes in front of his house until he heard about the reward your dad said he would give anyone who brought it back. But Larry didn't get the reward money 'cause he's the one who stole it in the first place. All Larry got was a lecture about stealing from your dad—who was good at giving lectures on stealing and other evil stuff 'cause he's the principal of the school you go to, and he does it every day professionally. He says lectures on evil are not his favorite part of his job.

Evil is killing six million people just because you don't like them, and it's not playing dodge ball with someone because you heard they were stupid and it might rub off on you. Instead, you just lean against the wall at recess and watch the girls have a contest for who can swing the highest so they can see into Mrs. Oliver's kitchen next to the school playground.

Evil is letting newborn babies die because they are mentally deficient or shaped funny or deaf and blind or have parts missing or parts that are the wrong size or shape, and it's sneaking off during a basketball game in junior high to smoke one cigarette between four or six people and telling your mom later that you were just watching or, "Yeah, I tried it just that one time but I didn't like it and I didn't inhale 'cause Don Hulin inhaled and it made him cough really hard." But smoking isn't that evil and, besides, God will forgive you at snow camp at Emerald Cove in March, or next September during the Torrey Memorial Bible Conference, whichever comes first. Smoking isn't evil; it's lying about it to your mom that's evil.

Evil is cheating on a test at school, and if it's a Bible test, it counts double against you.

Evil is lying about why you didn't get your homework done or taking off your clothes at the Tully Road Drive-In Theater (with a girl if you're a boy, or with a . . . well, you know) or getting some San Jose State University guys to buy you Boone's Creek wine at the Blossom Hill Liquor store or trying to buy one of those magazines with the naked lady pictures in it by hiding it in *Hot Rod* magazine when you go to pay for it, also at Blossom Hill Liquor 'cause it's closest to school and you can walk there. (Walking there isn't evil, it's what happens when you get there that's the evil part. If you just bought a PayDay candy bar or one of those small chocolate milks it would be okay to go to Blossom Hill Liquor any time you want. Or just getting the *Hot Rod* magazine without that other magazine inside it. I know all this because I went there with my dad one time, but he got a Snickers.)

Evil doesn't go away just because we grow up and as adults we "know better."

Evil is calling in sick to work when you're not really sick.

Evil is driving 75 miles per hour because you're late for church, or a movie, and if you drive the speed limit, everybody else whizzes by you and that's so embarrassing.

Evil is saying I love you when you don't really.

Evil is making people sit at the back of the bus just because their skin is darker than yours and that scares you. You let them vacuum the center aisle of your church before a wedding, but they cannot marry your daughter, or date her, or walk across campus holding hands with her. (Unless you get a note from your parents.)

Evil is Nazis, rapists, mass murderers, drunk drivers, terrorists, killers of baby seals, and killers of the buffalo who wander onto private land looking for something to eat in the winter when they can't find food in the National Park where they live most of the time.

Evil is the impatience of the driver behind you who honks his horn in the split second after the light has turned green and traffic has not begun to move immediately. (But I don't do it all the time.)

Evil is people who sell drugs to children and pimps and people who will say anything to get elected to political office, even things that they know are not completely true. It's better to tell the truth and lose than the other way around. And it's better to call your friend if you said you'd call, because if you don't, that's . . . well, you know.

Evil is what God hates, no matter who does it.

EXODUS

SECOND BOOK of the Old Testament. It's the story of the children of Israel leaving Egypt. Years later, actually centuries later, the Jews left Europe to reclaim their homeland, Israel. Eventually, both events were made into epic Hollywood movies.

Someday all of God's children will leave this earth and go to be with God in Heaven. That will be the biggest exodus ever. There will be plenty of people left in Hollywood to try and develop that into a movie as well. But it shouldn't be filmed "on location" in Des Moines.

FAITH

FAITH IS WHAT'S LEFT when there's nothing left.

Fish

IT USED TO BE A SECRET SIGN to identify Christians. They no longer have secret signs. Now they have neon signs.

And bumper stickers, T-shirts, bracelets, and every household item—all with a fish on them. (Most items also available with choice of cross or Star of David.)

"I just catch 'em and eat 'em. Don't ask me what they're called."

Forbidden Fruit

THE VERY FIRST NEIGHBORHOOD
ANYWHERE WAS EDEN. It was a garden paradise—the very first planned com-
munity. It had everything you could ask for in a great neighborhood:
flowers, organic vegetables, running water, well-manicured lawns,
waterfalls, pets, fruit trees, clear skies, sunshine, good schools, under-
ground utilities, and cable.

God asked Adam and Eve to live in Eden, enjoy themselves,
have lots of kids, and "stay away from the banana grove!"

Now there wasn't anything especially bad about bananas. God
just wanted to see whether Adam and Eve would obey instructions
or would decide for themselves what was best for them. God had
installed a new "program" in both Adam and Eve. It was called Free
Will 1.0, and this was the beta test. It allowed them to do whatever
they wanted to, whenever they wanted to. (*See* Free Will.)

One day Eve was out taking her early morning walk—Eve was a
morning person—when she met a banana salesman. They struck up
a conversation and before they knew it, it was lunchtime.

"Have you got any bananas here?" the salesman asked. "I'm
starving."

"Oh. Why, yes, we do," Eve said, "but, ah, God told us to stay
away from the banana tree and never ever to eat them. Wouldn't
you rather have a pomegranate or some homemade granola?"

"I don't think so," the salesman replied quickly.

"How about a nice, juicy, Yakima delicious apple?" Eve grinned.

45

N-o-o-o-o!" he roared, laughing at her. "I'm a banana man. If I don't have a couple of bananas every day, I'm just not myself. Ah! The smell of potassium in the morning."

"Oh," Eve was worried. "But God told us . . ."

"Horsefeathers!" The salesman's voice was now thundering through Eden, shaking the trees. "God just said that because he knew that if you climbed up into those bananas trees, you would be able to see the neighbor's garden and it's greener than Eden!"

"Neighbors?" Eve's curiosity was stirred. "I didn't know we had neighbors."

"Sure you do!" He continued to needle her. "And their garden is bigger, and better, and greener than Eden. And they get to eat all the bananas they want. God knows that if you eat any bananas, you would be as smart as he is. Then he wouldn't be able to boss you around anymore."

"Oh, I don't think God's bossy. My husband does, sometimes, but I find him quite pleasant." Eve was very confused, but what this salesman was saying was very, very interesting to her. "I find God very creative, don't you?"

"Sure, lady. He's a genius. Top of his class. Best of breed."

"You sure seem to know a lot about God and bananas." She had always been naturally inquisitive. "Do you know him?"

"Know him? Know him!" He could hardly contain himself. "I used to work for the guy. Why, lady, I was his No. 1 man. Then I discovered bananas! God kicked me out of his organization. I got too smart for him."

Well. Because Eve was curious about her neighbor's garden, and because they were very close to the banana grove and very hungry, and because Eve had tried all the other fruit in Eden, and because this salesman seemed very, very intelligent, and seemed to know what he was talking about, they went to the banana grove. Eve got so excited when she tried her first bite of banana that she forgot to climb up and look at the neighbor's garden. She just grabbed a big armload of bananas and hurried home to tell Adam about her amazing new discovery.

When Eve told Adam about the whole experience, she did not roar and prance about like the salesman. She just grabbed the biggest banana in the bunch, peeled it v-e-r-y slowly, and took a great big bite. Then she smiled a great big smile and held it up to Adam's mouth . . . and . . . Adam smiled . . . and . . . took a great big bite, too.

"Fantastic!" Adam announced with great delight. "Amazing." And, oh what happened next was rich. It was like a party. Adam and Eve began peeling and eating all of the bananas that Eve had brought home.

"WHAT'S GOING ON HERE?" A great big voice resounded like an earthquake rumbling through Eden, shaking every leaf and limb in the Garden. Even the rocks trembled. Everything with feet or wings rushed for cover.

Adam and Eve knew that it was God's voice and that he was very mad. They immediately dropped all of their bananas and started running for a place to hide. While they were running, they slipped and fell on all the empty banana peels.

That's where God caught up with them, lying in a mountain of evidence. God told Adam and Eve that they would have to leave the

Garden of Eden because they had disobeyed him.

Today people are still slipping because they, too, want to be as smart as God.

49

How long at current address? Yr. _____ Mo. _____ *Forever.*

WHAT GOD WRITES on a questionnaire or an application when they ask, "How long at current address?"

(free will)

FREE WILL IS THE REASON the world is the way it is, mostly. We've made it that way through our choices. When Claude Monet put brush in hand and painted his glorious *Water Lilies,* it was as much an act of free will as when another person puts a gun in their hand and uses their free will to choose violence.

God made the hand.

We have used our hands to heal and to hurt. It's our choice. We make hundreds of choices a day. Many times there have been opportunities to heal and we have kept our hands in our pockets.

If God wanted to stop us from doing violence with our hands, he should have deprogramed Adam and Eve right after those first few bites of the forbidden banana. Or God should never have let us invent pockets.

God enjoys our love. But God did not rig the game of life or wire our hearts and minds so we can only love our Creator.

Rather it is our choice to love and serve God, just as it is our choice to love, respect, and care for each other. Even strangers.

We choose our friends, our lovers, our paintbrushes, and our lifestyle. We can choose to help others or ignore their needs. We can choose to pick, peel, and clean carrots out of our garden and share them with those who do not have a vegetable garden.

Every once in a while, have your kids use their thumbs for finger painting instead of video games.

We can choose our weapons—the pistol, or the pen.

Frogs

WHEN GOD HAS A MESSAGE TO DELIVER, he always sends the best messenger for the job. Sometimes God sends angels, sometimes prophets, one time God sent frogs. These were not magic frogs or talking frogs; they were just lots of frogs. Lots and lots and lots and lots and lots of frogs.

God also sent plagues of gnats, flies, dead cattle, boils, hail, locusts, darkness, and death of every first-born son of every family.

They got the message.

G is for gravy, which is never mentioned in the Bible

"G" IS ALSO
FOR GOD.

God is mentioned in the Bible. A lot. I think you knew that. Do you know God?

THAT WAS THE ORIGINAL NAME for the third planet from the Sun. When the solar system was brand new, God had a name and a place for everything. Mars was called "the smallish red thing." Saturn was "a different kind of gases, a different kind of planet." Venus was named "girls only." Pluto was called "where we keep the ice." Uranus was to be called "Dodger Stadium," but, alas, that name was already registered.

But Earth was the *Garden* or "The Place Where We Grow Everything." It was the planet of life—more life than any place else. It was here that God would develop roses, banded milk snakes, pelicans, pandas, prisms, propellers, pollen, protective eyewear, pine trees, pickles, and place kickers. Here, too, humankind would multiply—and divide—and discover hash brown potatoes, the telegraph, insulation, anesthesiology, and musical comedy.

Garden. That's what it started out as. That's what it was meant to be all along. But we humans came along with our own ideas—our own choices—of what this place could be. Many of our ideas were grand, but some were not helpful for keeping the Garden a garden.

Maybe somewhere there's a garden with no pollution. The fish can see where they're going, and the birds don't cough. There you can sit all day, all week, and never hear a car horn honking impatiently or the wail of an anxious ambulance.

What you will hear are dogs barking, water falling, and babies crying. They're not tired or hungry or in pain. They're just very happy to be in the Garden.

ALL CHILDREN ARE GIFTED. They are born gifted. Given special qualities by their Creator that make them uniquely who they are—unlike anyone else. Just ask the mother of twins or triplets: no two children are exactly alike. Each of us are different. Special. This specialness is the Creator's gift.

But along the way, we keep giving children more and more presents and taking away their gifts.

Goats

TRUE FAITH SEPARATES the sheep from the goats, Jesus said. In church, though, the goats are invited. Not everyone who goes to church is a true believer. Some may be seeking or thinking about seeking a personal faith. Many churches have taken to calling these folks "seekers."

Many just come to take a peek at what goes on in church. These are called "peekers." Both seekers and peekers are met at the church door by greeters who turn them over to seaters. But neither seekers nor peekers are followers yet. Jesus called his followers "sheep." Seekers and peekers are still in their pre-sheep phase. For now, they are goats.

Some will remain goats for a long, long time. Many become professional goats—like Madeleine Muray Goathair. (*See* Atheist.)

Jesus referred to himself as our shepherd. (*See* Shepherd.)

If you ever go to a church where there are no goats or they don't allow goats, it is not a real church. Some churches allow goats once a year during the March Goat Round-Up Days. But a church

without goats might actually be a golf course or a political action committee or a place that used to be a church but is now just putting on a weekly show and looks a lot like church. They might even still sing songs out of a book.

But no goats, no church. If your church has no goats, or very few goats, bring one next Sunday just for fun. And to confuse everybody even further, sit in the front row. It is almost always empty.

Maybe God has been saving those front seats for goats, just in case they want a peek.

59

Godot

(Enters from stage left)
Have you been waiting long?

GODOT MAY BE THE MOST FAMOUS CHARACTER in a play that never, ever, appears on stage. In Samuel Beckett's play, *Waiting for Godot,* two characters wait on an empty stage—except for a lone, leafless tree.

Everyone who has ever seen, read or even heard of *Waiting for Godot* inevitably gets around to the "who is Godot" question. Irish playwright Samuel Beckett, who invented Godot, says—adamantly—that Godot is not God.

I agree. Godot is not God. I think that most folks, like the characters in Beckett's play—and maybe Beckett himself—are going on with their lives while at the same time waiting for the ever-tardy Godot. They are waiting for the next big thing to unravel all the mysteries of life—well, at least their life.

It's as if we are all living on the day in-between Good Friday when Jesus was nailed to a leafless tree and the day he rose from the dead. So here we are, waiting, for, well, whatever is next.

CONCEPT SELDOM PUT INTO PRAC-TICE. It is some-thing preached that is rarely practiced. Too often we stand between the God of grace and the people who need that remarkable gift the most.

We seem to be saying, "Yes, you can have this wonderful free gift, but first we'd like you to attend our ten-week "Preparation-for-Receiving-Grace" class. Then we need you to sign one of our "I'm-Really-Really-Sorry-for-What-I-Did" certificates and attend the "How-to-Act-Like-a-Long-Time-Church-Goer" workshop. Then you can take off the sweatshirt we gave you with the big red "S" on the front.

GREED

Everyone wants to go to

Heaven

but no one wants
to buy a ticket.

SOME PEOPLE BELIEVE IN HELL SOME PEOPLE DON'T. SOMEDAY, THEY WILL.

HOBBY

HAVING A HOBBY is an excellent way to take a break from your normal day-to-day routine. It can be fun to have a hobby even if your routine isn't routine.

Some people have collections of seashells, postage stamps of the world, old books, or every known household necessity with Mickey Mouse on it. My friend's mother developed an early fascination for frog figurines. She has collected enough to fill her house with frogs—over two hundred pieces. Her home is frogful. She's been collecting since just after frogs were invented. It should be noted that she is happy and healthy. She just likes frogs.

Having a hobby is a sign that you are finding pleasure and enjoyment in life. A psychologist friend of mine wrote a book on how to have fun after you have been in recovery from some life-crippling addiction or personal trauma. She says that having a hobby shows that you are on the path to a full, rich, rewarding existence.

I collect political campaign buttons (600), rubber stamps (226), and hats (283), and have a snowballing stock of cheap airport snow globes (a few dozen). It may be instructive to note that if you have three of anything that is not a personal or household necessity, you are officially a collector of that item. For the record I have three mechanical, cymbal-clanging, battery-operated monkeys. I am on the road to total wellness.

H⊘PE

HOPE IS NOT WHEN YOU CLOSE YOUR EYES and blow out
all the candles on your birthday cake and hope for a pony (when
you're a child) or a Mustang, later.

Hope is not crossing your fingers while taking a test in school
hoping you'll magically remember stuff you never studied.

Hope is when you come to the end of your abilities and you
don't know where to turn. You feel tested beyond your limits. You
feel like you are standing on the edge of a dark abyss, afraid to
jump. If you put your trust in God, one of two things will happen
when you jump: there will be someone there to catch you, or you
will be taught how to fly!

IMPOSSIBLE

THE ONLY ASSIGNMENTS that God will handle personally. With all others, he asks us, "What are you going to do about that?"

Once upon a time

It all started with

the first thing that happened was

On the very first day At the start of
To begin with we the beginning was

At the beginning

In

In the beginning

~~In the beginning~~

IN THE BEGINNING

WHEN GOD–WHO LIVED "IN THE BEGINNING"–decided to get it all going, Moses, an old friend of God's, suggested that they should write some of it down. "So we won't forget it," Moses explained.

"That's a great idea, Moses. Why don't you do that?"

Moses was not a very good speaker, but as it turned out, he was a pretty good scribbler.

To get him started, God jotted down a few notes from the very beginning, and gave them to Moses–since Moses was not actually "in the beginning."

(What follows is a rare copy of one of God's earliest memos to Moses.)

From the desk of **J. Hovah God**

Date: I am
From: God
To: Moishe
Re: In the beginning

It all started with what seemed like a pretty good idea at the time: spheres of color and light swirling through space (we had lots of space back then). All with a deep blue background. A little gas, a few minerals, and several barrels of water (which we made ourselves). Add piles of dirt.

Directions for making type 1 dirt: 1.) Take everything; 2.) Grind it down as fine as possible: 3.) Repeat step two: 4.) Spread it around everywhere: 5.) Don't track it into the house on your mother's new beige carpet or you'll never hear the end of it.

Dirt. That was a wonderfully useful development. (We had a lot of ground to cover.) We all took a week off to work on it. And it worked great! The first thing we made was light—lots of light—so we could see what we were doing and so we wouldn't put everything in the same place and so everything wouldn't bump into each other. Light was good. Light may be my favorite thing—other than children.

If I were ever to change my name, I'd probably go by "Light." (Every time I hear one of you say, "Hey, lighten up!" I feel like you're really saying, "Hey, be more like the Creator.")

We made a gazillion and a half categories of plants and animals next. Botanists and zoologists were developed much later to explain it all. (I just wanted you to enjoy it first.)

Now, when I say something was "good" what I mean was it worked. In most cases it worked as well as we thought it would.

As for how much time it took us to do all this, that's not really important. Just write that we did it in six phases, kind of like your days. What is important is that we did it. We did everything, even though some things took longer than I thought, while other things didn't take as long as you might imagine. Once we figured out the "life" thing, we used it on everything. (Even a few places you don't know about yet.)

Finally we made man. No, I mean we made humans. No, I mean "man." That was good! Then we made woman. That was good too—in some ways woman was better. (Don't take that personally, Mo.)

Man and woman hit it off pretty well right from the start. (Turns out they had very similar tastes.) We purposely made them comparable, though not alike. It was only when they started trying to be more and more alike that much of the trouble began.

That should cover the first couple of chapters, Mo. I know your writing style will dress it up so it's more interesting to read than my pterodactyl scratchings. We can fill in any missing details in the second draft. And don't worry about precise measurements, this isn't science, it's creation.

When we finished phase six, we all took a day off to walk around for a while and just enjoy it! (Remind me to show you my favorite view and the best darn swimming hole on the planet.)

G

P.S. Hope this all makes some sort of sense to you. I hate to type, and English was not my first language.

A SECRET LANGUAGE. Short phrases and special words or clichés that we use as a shortcut in communications. As often as not they are a roadblock that keep us from expressing real thoughts and authentic feelings. Next time, put it in your own words.

"Jesus in Wonderland!"

WHAT IF GOD CAME TO EARTH AND WALKED AMONG US? What if that has already happened?

The Jesus found in the New Testament, many believe, was the Creator come among us. I have often wondered if God had any idea of just what he was getting himself into by coming to Earth.

This next section is, therefore, titled "Jesus in Wonderland," wherein we take a squint-eyed peek at an incident or two that the writers of the four syncopated gospels may have neglected to tell us about.

For example, one event shows what might happen if Jesus were to visit us today and stop by a religious television station. What might we expect him to do?

"I start with two Galilean trout. If you are serving more than 10,000, just double everything."

JOHN WAS JESUS' COUSIN. His first cousin. At least he was the first cousin of the Jesus that we are told about. John's father was a priest, but John became a preacher anyway. His headquarters was in a wilderness area outside the city—waterfront property. John did not preach in a church. He was an "evangelist." (Do not see "E.")

John did not have his own television show. His favorite saying was, "Hey! Watch out, 'cause God's coming!"

His favorite outdoor sport was dunking people in the Jordan River. The people being dunked wanted to show everybody that they were changing their lives. (*See* Under New Management.) Dunking symbolized an end to their old, selfish ways and a beginning of a brand new life—guided by their Creator.

Because of all this dunking, John was given a nickname that has stuck all these years. He was called John the Dunker.

Ever since then, people have used this name for all kinds of religious organizations: the Southern Dunkers Convention, First Dunken

Church, the General Association of Regular Dunkers, the Dunkers General Conference, Swedish Dunkers, American Dunkers, and Dunkin' Doughnuts.

A lot of people are still getting dunked today, for pretty much the same reason as John the Dunker first intended. Some people dunk their whole body underwater using a lake, an ocean, or a swimming pool. Some churches even have a specially designed, built-in dunkistry—right up in the front of the church.

Other dunkers just sprinkle a little water on the top of their head, a splash behind each ear, or dab a drop here and there on special trouble spots. Fanatics stand in the church parking lot and give themselves a thorough hosing. How and where the dunking happens is not important. Nor is the amount of water used on each person important.

When we get to Heaven, St. Peter will not be checking for a certain number of water marks. Promise.

"Jokes!"

TWO BABYLONIANS WALK INTO A BAR . . .

The first motorcycle found in the Bible is when *Joshua's Triumph was heard throughout the land.* This is a Bible joke. The first phone number in the Bible is *Adam 8-1-2.* The first tennis match was when *David served in Saul's court.* Church people seem to be constantly making up Bible jokes for church summer camp, church social gatherings, or one of the too many giant "be-kind-to-God" festivals or super-duper youth gatherings. Some believe that such jokes are effective in convincing teenagers and other tough audiences that God is cool and will not bite. Mostly these Bible jokes are not all that funny, but are designed to make the listener believe that church people are normal too, and not as weird, by half, as what is thought. (While, on the other hand, some church folk are twice as weird as you might suspect.)

As it happens, the Bible is filled with humor. Jesus used humor as a key tool in his teaching, like the time Jesus noticed a guy pointing out a little tiny speck of dirt in another guy's eye.

"Hey!" Jesus said, "Before you point out that speck of dirt in another person's left eye, you'd better remove that 2' x 4' plank of pine from your own pupil, Popeye. Only then will you be able to see clearly their urgent need." Jesus pointed out this guy's judgemental hypocrisy.

And the crowd roared. They got the joke.

Most of us are pretty good at finding fault (and tiny specks of dirt) in others—especially when they have the same problems that we do. Jesus spotted the man with the lumber in his eye because Jesus had nothing in his eyes and because the man with the 2' x 4' in his eye had a guilty conscience and a big mouth. No joke.

"Jokes" 2

WHENEVER THE SUBJECT OF "HUMOR AND GOD" COMES UP, people get nervous. They fear that we are going to make fun of God. Instead we merely want to notice and enjoy God's sense of humor. God is and always has been funny. You need look no further than your local zoo or employee lunchroom. Better yet, take a peek in your local bathroom mirror.

God's humor is found in both the Older and Newer Testaments of the Bible. Trying to read the stories and teachings of Jesus as strictly serious stuff is not possible. His wit, like ours, does not have to be blasphemous. But the traditionally held atmosphere of somber pondering of the Bible's teachings makes Jesus gloomy, scary even. He was anything but. Jesus' humor was serious business.

In Matthew's gospel of Jesus, he writes, "Do not look dismal." (Matt. 6:16.) Still we seem unable to hear the tragedy of the crucifixion of Jesus and also embrace a laughing, humorous Jesus. We make the "sad picture the whole picture." (Elton Trueblood, *The Humor of Christ,* Harper & Row, 1964.) Even the great theologian, Soren "Klass Klown" Kierkegaard, observed that a well-placed humorous comment will always be a bit profound. Jesus shed real tears at the death of his friend Lazarus. Later it is that same Jesus who also suggests shoving a camel through the eye of a needle. (*See* Camel.) These emotions are contrary, but they are not contradictory. It is because religious people are so relentlessly somber and sober, even boring, that they are all too often so unattractive to people out side of a relationship with their Creator.

Jesus was liked by those who met him and not because he was a party pooper. He did not begin any of his legendary talks the way far too many church youth groups I've visited begin: "All right now, people, let's settle down, time to get serious."

Any teaching of the life of Jesus that leaves out his levity would be distorted. In other words, a picture of a humorless Jesus is not completely true.

To miss his punchline is to miss his message. But we do that a lot.

ONE OF THE FIRST BIBLE STORIES any kid learns in Sunday school is the amazing story of Jonah. We all knew it was about salvation. God gave Jonah a second chance when Jonah went the wrong way.

It's the same second chance that God gives each of us when our pride and selfishness sends our own lives down the wrong fork in the road. It is a second chance that we mostly do not deserve and certainly have not earned. God has given that second chance a name—grace.

As I got older and my friends started going to seminary, I learned that the story of Jonah is really about the accurate identification of fish.

NOT EVERYONE who kisses you is your friend.

KNOWLEDGE

EINSTEIN SAID, "Imagination is more powerful than knowledge."
What an imagination that Albert had.

I AM CONVINCED that there will be lots of laughter in Heaven. Start practicing now, so you won't feel left out.

THE LAW OF GOD IS PERFECTION. (*See* Perfection.)

Why does God have to be so strict?

In a football game, you have to get the ball over the goal line to score a touchdown. Maybe it should be enough if you play fairly well and get the ball near the line. Why do you always have to get the ball *over* the line?

Wouldn't a loving God be more flexible—more understanding? Anybody who has been pretty good or near good or sort of good . . . picky, picky, picky.

Leadership

JESUS SAID, "A CHILD WILL LEAD YOU."

He did not mention that we must be willing to be led.

"We fired our youth minister tonight. He's been secretly dating one of the high school girls. I was the lone dissenting vote. The senior pastor told me to go home and pray about my attitude."

"I stopped here at Clancy's for a beer first."

A LEPER IS SOMEONE with a very bad sickness—leprosy. It used to be that if you were a leper, you were not allowed live in a regular house. Lepers were forced to live in special "Lepers Only" neighborhoods outside big cities.

Today not only lepers, but other people as well, are kept out of neighborhoods. They are kept out because they are different. They are kept out because they have a different color skin, or are diagnosed with mental retardation or because they are physically handicapped. Some people think that anyone who is different is not "normal."

But the people who ostracize others from "normal" neighborhoods have a sickness that is worse than leprosy. They have ignorance. And it's very, very contagious.

LOCAL CRITIC

MRS. ALFRED "MINA" BECKMAN, GREETING HER pastor Rev. Harold "Hap" Brahams, following the 11:15 A.M. Sunday worship service, explained that she was not in her usual third row, left side (facing the pulpit), on the center aisle seat, at the 9:30 service because her nephew, Teddy Rosenquist-Ghormley, was sick and unable to pick her up at 8:45 as usual, so she got a ride with her neighbors, the Haneys, who prefer the "late service" so they can get to Beadles Cafeteria at 12:30, which is just after the breakfast buffet has been shut down and the salad bar has opened—with the hot bacon dressing for the spinach salad—which gives Mrs. Haney heartburn, but she only gets it once a week so her gerontologist, Dr. Emile Heinecker, says it's all right.

"And I thought the sopranos were a bit flat this morning, didn't you? Well, I'd love to stop and chat, but . . ."

Love Letter

ONE OF THE MANY PLACES that received mail from the Apostle Paul (a.k.a. Saint Paul, a.k.a. Lefty, a.k.a. the Mailman, and a.k.a. Mr. Picky) was the church in a Greek town named Corinth. Paul once wrote them a love letter. That is to say, he wrote them a letter about love—as God sees it. Among other things, Paul told all the believers in Corinth that love does not keep an account of the evil done by others.

This would be like when you refuse to help a friend move her big, old, heavy piano 'cause she wouldn't let you borrow her rototiller when you were turning your front yard into a "zero-scape," low-water, high-tolerance garden. Paul didn't speak English, but if he had, maybe he would have just written to his friends in Corinth and said, "Holding a grudge is not love. Love is an unexpected breath of fresh air, a cool and constant breeze. Love is not a full nelson."

Love is also not a list on a pull-down menu on your laptop computer. This handy list reminds you of every little thing you've done for *him* and everything he has *not* done for you. (Select Edit menu; click Undo.) Create a new memo titled "Love." In the "to do" column, use your mouse to double-click on "give it away."

LOVE YOUR ENEMY

It will drive 'em nuts !

MEDIOCRITY

GOD'S STANDARD IS PERFECTION. The human standard these days is "okay" or "that'll be fine" or "not bad." When God created the earth, he didn't make any mediocre mountains, okay oceans, or so-so seagulls soaring slowly above. Creation contains no moderate moose. Although many moose may be middle-of-the-road. Nor did the Creator tell the blazing sun, just as it reached mid-blaze, "That'll do star, that'll do."

Mostly we do not expect each other to be blazing, but every time someone does blaze, avoiding mediocrity, it encourages others to be fully themselves also. "Perfect" does not mean flawless. According to the indefatigable Madeleine L'Engle (author of *A Wrinkle in Time*), reading from the *Oxford Dictionary*, "perfect" means "to do thoroughly." Be thoroughly dazzling today. And tomorrow, too, if you're up to it.

MICAH

PROPHET OF GOD.

The Bible is full of stories about prophets and what they said. Most of the time it was not good news.

Micah worked at Doom & Gloom, Inc. Like his friend Isaiah, Micah didn't even want the job of being the prophet of God. It's no fun—not for the prophet and especially not for the people being propheted at.

That was the old days.

Today there are prophets, too. Lots and lots of prophets—or so it seems.

The prophets of today are nothing like Micah. These new prophets seem to enjoy saying scary, terrible things. They write lots of books, make videotapes, and do their prophet act on television. Day and night. This is quite different from the old way (the Old Testament way) of just speaking the one message God gave them and then going back to their regular job as night manager at Wal-Mart.

Jesus said that someday many will speak in God's name, but not be sent from God. Jesus called these people "false prophets."

If you ever meet someone on the street or hear someone on television or at a big religious meeting who says he or she is a prophet sent with a message from God, listen very closely to everything that person says. If their message is different from what God tells us in the Bible, then you have probably met a false prophet—maybe even a banana salesman.

[Behind too many of today's self-made prophets is the profit motive.]

MIRACLES

LOOK AT YOUR HAND. Right now. Both sides. See the miracle?

MOSES

LEADER OF HIS PEOPLE, ex-shepherd, ex-leader of someone else's people.

Moses discovered that a career shift or two late in life isn't such a bad thing.

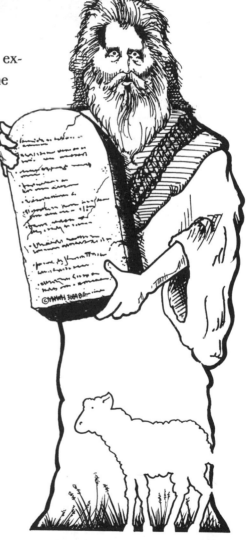

THE BUILDING BLOCK OF LIFE. (Let it dry first, before you try to build anything with it. Fresh, wet mud is fairly difficult to build with, unless you're God.)

It was mud that God rolled around in his hands and used to make Adam.

Later, Jesus used mud (following an old family recipe calling for dirt mixed with saliva) to make blind Bartimaeus see 20/20.

With all the mud around everywhere, it's a wonder that only God and children have found a good use for it.

Nationality? Place of origin. Ethnic background. (Check only one)

MY NATIONALITY? Well, let's see, on my mother's side it's mostly Hebrew kings and prostitutes. On my birth father's side, we go way, way back.

NiMROD!

THERE ONCE WAS A KING NAMED NIMROD. He had big ideas. One of his ideas was the biggest idea anyone had ever had. So far. He summoned his royal architects and gave them a very tall order. "Build me a tower to Heaven so I can see God, face-to-face." Nimrod and his tower didn't quite make it to Heaven. (*See* Babel.)

Ever since then, kids everywhere, when their playmate or older sibling barks out a foolish order—treating the littler kid like a servant—will say, "Oh, don't be such a Nimrod!"

THE BIBLE HAS LOTS OF NUMBERS IN IT:

1 great big fish (*See* Jonah.)

2 guards at Parbar

3 Magi (*See* Wisemen)

4 horsemen

5 loaves of bread served with two fresh Galilean rainbow trout sautéed in fume blanc with a dill reduction on a bed of couscous

6 days of Creation

7 seals (trained)

8 maids a-milking

9 lepers

10 Commandments

11 faithful apostles

12 baskets full of leftovers (*See* No. 5 above)

969 years (the age of the oldest person who ever lived—so far.)

Some of the numbers in the Bible are so big that only words like "multitude" and "host" can be used. The Bible has a multitude of Heavenly hosts.

But the highest number in the Bible started when God promised Abraham that he would be the father with the most children.

That was how the nation of Israel began. Abraham's children were the Children of God. Now everyone who chooses to follow Jesus becomes a child of God—and of Abraham.

So how many children does Abraham have? They're still counting.

123456789

SOME PEOPLE WILL TELL YOU that original sin was what happened in the garden of Eden when Adam and Eve disobeyed God and ate the forbidden fruit. (*See* Forbidden Fruit.)

Original sin actually means you did it. It originated with you. You will be judged for what you did—not for what your parents did. It isn't Adam's fault, or the month you were born, or where you lived as a child.

It's all yours. You did it.

And I'm telling.

Owners Manual

WHAT IF YOU DON'T BELIEVE
IN THE BIBLE? Fine. There are
lots of other books wherein you
might find a god that is more to
your liking. The world is full of many different teachings. When
you do find a book that seems to suit you better than the Bible,
ask the god you find there to take care of world suffering.

For many, the Bible is the owner's manual for human behavior and belief. It is not a science textbook, though true science
seems more and more to align its thinking with the Bible's obser-
vations.

As an owner's manual, the Bible has proven to be an effective resource for thousands of people across all cultural and eth-
nic boundaries. What all these people have in common is their
peopleness. The adultery and deceit practiced by King David
and his rooftop girlfriend and neighbor, Bathsheba, was no different—emotionally and psychologically—than adultery practiced
by men and women, movie stars, and monarchs of today. The
Bible is a book about people, for people.

If you drive a Chevy, you probably were provided an
owner's manual from the manufacturer that is all about
Chevrolet. General Motors, maker of all Chevrolet cars, would
not think of giving you an owner's manual for Toyota, John

Deer, or Macintosh. It would not fit. But maybe you don't think your Chevy manual covers all the subjects that interest you. So drive your Chevy Malibu over to the Land Rover shop nearest you, hand them the Macintosh G4 manual under your front seat, and say, "Fix it."

Good luck.

Maybe they'll have a Bible in the customer lounge for you to read during your very long wait.

THE QUESTION IS OFTEN ASKED, if God is love then why is there pain and suffering in the world? Why are there children dying of starvation and disease that ravages entire nations? Wouldn't a God of love prevent this from happening or at least put a stop to it when it does?

God may be asking the same questions:

"I've given the human race science, medicine, agriculture, air travel, refrigeration, so why do you allow so many to go malnourished and disease ridden? Why does anyone die of starvation? But I know, too, that I also gave you free will to do just as you please.

"Help the suffering, please."

PARIS

THE BROCHURE
READ, "Gospel Tour.
Walk where Jesus walked!" Maybe there are different stops on this
tour where they have the hands and footprints of Jesus—like that
famous Chinese Theater in Hollywood. You could compare your
shoe size (or sandal size) to Jesus.

The brochure went on to list all the places your gospel tour
would visit, just like Jesus visited: the Holy Land, Greece, Egypt,
Italy, Germany, and Paris, France! I think Jesus went there once on
a family vacation or a Sabbath school convention.

You can send off your registration forms and go on the "30 Bible
Hot Spots in 10 Days" tour. Jerusalem, Bethlehem, Ur, Nazareth,
Jericho, Cairo, Rome, Athens, Paris, and six other cities of the Bible.

Lots of church folk believe you can justify any activity if a Bible
study is thrown in for validation. Church youth group beach trips
and backyard swim and bar-be-que parties are all deemed okey
dokey, just as long as a devotional—no matter how brief—is squeezed
into the agenda somewhere. It usually only amounts to our Pastor
Ed (Holt) retelling a Bible story that we all knew, backward and for-
ward, and a joke or story about some silly thing his old Sunday
school teacher told him when Pastor Ed was our age. Then a quick
prayer, ending in, "Amen. Everybody in the pool!"

There was a big controversy one year when Pastor Ed did the
devotional with most of us still in the pool: on inflatable mats, wearing inner tubes, perched on the diving board. Even Pastor Ed sat on

the edge of the pool with his feet in the water while he told a well-known Bible story.

People in our church talked about that little bump in the theological parking lot for years!

It really is okay with God for us to visit gay Pairee, even if Jesus never did. Heck, our family went back to Le Sueur, Minnesota, every other summer to see the Easterlands, the Iversons, and the Mootz's. Jesus has never been there as far as anyone in Le Sueur can remember.

Jesus has also never been anywhere in North America, or if he has, somebody has been keeping awfully quiet about it for a very long time. (*See* Jesus in Wonderland.)

He should have left a note, or maybe his feet prints in the cement next to someone's swimming pool.

PARKING

THERE IS NO PARKING PROBLEM in Heaven because there are no cars. No cars, no problem.

Meanwhile, back here on Earth, in the Bible, Jesus says that wherever two or more are gathered two-gether in his name there will be a parking problem and an argument.

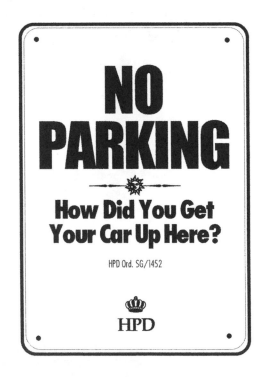

ANY PLACE WHERE GOD IS at the very center. God is whispering, "Shhhhhh. Listen."

If we don't hear anything or we don't understand, that's peace. Real peace, God says, can only be found beyond that place we call Understanding.

Perfection

A LOT OF PEOPLE WORRY about all this talk in church about perfection. No one is perfect. The dictionary says it means to be "complete, sound, thorough" and mentions something in passing about being "flawless."

Maybe we can't be flawless, but we could be a bit more thorough. We could finish our commitments, keep our promises, and complete broken relationships. We could clean out the garage or the basement. Nah.

If all else fails, we could just stay home and leave everyone else alone.

PIPE SMOKE
Of fine tobacco & finer points of theology

I AM A PIPE SMOKER. (Though technically the fragrant China Black tobacco in my pipe does all the smoking. I am merely a sucker.) I purchased my first pipe at the tobacco shop on Main Street, USA, Disneyland.

I first became fascinated with pipe smoking watching Basil Rathbone as Sherlock Holmes. Then later in photographs and, more importantly, from the writings of C. S. Lewis and G. K. Chesterton (a personal favorite). Pipe smokers, both wrote on the silliness of American church folk who believe it to be sinful.

It is thirty years since I bought that first pipe as a birthday present to myself at eighteen. These days I smoke infrequently. As I write this, I have not lit up in more than eight weeks. I enjoy it, but I am not addicted to it. I'm not, really. No really, I'm not. I could give it up anytime.

Once, during a Q&A session at a Crhistian college, after one of my one-man plays, a student offered, "I heard that you smoke a pipe."

"Yes, I do." I answered.

"Well, ah, the Bible says that the body is the temple of the Holy Spirit." He was not, it seemed to me, being judgemental, just curious. "Aren't we supposed to keep our bodies pure? Doesn't smoking a pipe go against that?"

"No." I let my quick response hang for a moment. "Should I explain?" Many nodded.

"In the passage you refer to (I Corinthians 6:9), the Apostle Paul is writing about the sexual immorality of certain temple priests, hence the temple allusion. We in the more uptight American wing of Christianity have broadened Paul's argument to cover smoking, drinking, and, on this campus, dancing. Paul never said any such thing. In fact, he said all sins are "outside the body." Read it for yourself. And your question reveals your ignorance on the art of pipe smoking. We pipe smokers do *not* inhale. Ergo, the smoke never enters the temple. It stays in the narthex, the outer lobby, during the entire experience. My temple remains inviolate."

Much laughter and applause followed, most vigorously from the off-campus Cigarettes at Midnight in the Parking Lot of Pizza Palace Smoking Club.

"But," I went on,"what about we sugar and caffeine addicts? Are we to be spared the wrath of the Pure Temple Committee? And leave us not forget the mind-numbing pages of *People* magazine? I could go on, but . . ."

Often, in our zeal to preserve the purity of God's image through an artificially flawless lifestyle, we are curiously selective in the targets of our temple-cleansing efforts.

Jesus said that what we eat goes through us and "out the drain." He meant our personal drain. There he goes again with more potty humor. What has *he* been smoking?

Prayer

CONVERSATION. SOUNDS EASY. Most of us tend to forget that conversation means listening as well as talking. Usually when we think about prayer, we think about praying to God.

Some people pray *at* God or at other people (who are in the room at the time) while pretending to be praying to God.

You can pray anywhere. Inside or outside. In the dark, on the run, at a movie, underwater, with a friend, alone, or even in a church basement. You can even pray at school, whenever you want to. You don't need a flagpole, a group of friends, or permission from the government.

A lot of folks pray at bedtime—like when your mom used to say, "Brush your teeth, turn off your lights, say your prayers, and turn off your stereo."

Sometimes we pray before we eat. (Except at McDonald's, where you just scratch your head, stare at your fries, and mumble, "Thanks, God.")

Usually, though, we pray when we want something badly or we are in pain. (*See* YHWH.)

Other times we pray when we don't know what else to do and can't even think of what to say to God. Maybe we are lonely. But "lonely" expresses a feeling that somebody has already felt, only we do not want to call our feeling what someone else has already called it. We want to make up our own name for our problem. Our very own, brand-new, never-before-spoken language. Like "AUGH!" or "Y-R-R-B!" or even "F-DL-TH-TH-M!"

That's a perfectly acceptable way to pray because God speaks all languages: American, Urdu, Swahili, Mexican, French, Amheric, Flemish, baby talk, Japanese, Qetzal, Hmong, Gaelic, Braille, jive, Southern Methodist, Armenian, and Elfan. God even understands Seminary Professor.

No matter which language you use to talk, sing, whisper, think, feel, yell, or pray, God listens. And God answers. Always.

Don't forget to listen back.

Preacher

(Beginning sermon. Big voice)

"My sermon this morning is from the second chapter of my new book. Copies available, for sale, at the back. Now, let us close in prayer. 'Our father . . .'"

PRIDE

A LOT OF PEOPLE GO ON DIETS in the spring so they'll look good in their summer swimwear. They go to the beach and develop a golden tan that makes them feel pretty good about themselves (at least on the outside). They lost all that weight and got skinny and tan. They're pretty darn proud of themselves all summer. In the Bible we were warned about this where it says "pride cometh before the fall." (Proverbs 16:18.)

Quaker

ANY FRIEND of God's is a friend of mine.

QUICK

AS IN FAST. Right now! And, "Hey, that wasn't there a minute ago."

The Bible tells of special messengers from God—angels. On only a few occasions does the Bible tell us their names: Michael, Gabriel Aerial, Low ("and Low, the angel of the Lord, came upon them." Luke 2), and Suddenly (as in "Suddenly the angel of God was in their midst." Acts 12).

Seems like there's not much in the Bible that happens slowly.

FOR A GOOD TIME contact Rahab.com. She was a professional date. Her business card said, "Available for dinner most nights of the week."

She was a working girl.

One day some guys came to town. They had been sent there by God (and Joshua) to check the place out—the town, not Rahab's apartment. They needed her help though. It seems they were spies sent by the soon-to-be-attacking army of Israel. When local officials caught wind that there may be spies in town (apparently they were all wearing this strong cologne named Channel No. 007), the local authorities went on a house-to-house search for these fragrant for-eign intruders.

Rahab's apartment, as good fortune would have it, was built into the massive (and very thick) city walls. Arriving at Rahab's place, the investigating soldiers did not bang angrily on the door. Most of them knew Rahab from . . . well, you get to know everybody when you're in law enforcement, you know. In this town, *everybody* knew Rahab.

"Hi, boys." Always her first words to anyone that came to her door. "Oh, don't you just love a man in uniform? I do. What brings you fellas to this part of the wall in the middle of the afternoon?"

"We're lookin' for spies," the gruff sergeant barked, pretending to be official and not to have noticed the lovely, form-fitting, diaphanous chemise that Rahab had thrown on to answer the door.

"I'd love to help you look, fellas, but I got company right this minute—if you know what I mean," she said with a wink, leaning out of the doorway to show off her as-yet-unremarked-upon scarlet bed clothing.

"Who you got in there, Rahab?" The sergeant demanded in unconvincing indignation.

"Is it a spy?" One of the younger soldiers interrogated from the back of the pack.

"A spy? How should I know? Who checks IDs anymore. His shekels were the same color as anyone else's. I'd invite you back for some home-brewed ice tea later, but I've got back-to-back bookings through supper time. Time is money, boys,"

"Aw, we trust you, Rahab, but we gotta at least knock on every door."

"Yeah, we got a checklist, Miss Rahab," came the voice of an eager young recruit, fresh out of the academy.

"She don't care about no checklist, Shem!" a bigger, older soldier snapped.

"Sorry to bother you, Rahab." The sergeant was now quite conciliatory, even smiling.

"No bother boys. Stop by anytime. I'm always here."

As the door closed, the spies exhaled a long sigh of relief. They had been hiding under a stack of firewood in the corner.

140

"Quickly!" She said quickly. "Grab that rope on the floor in the corner and come with me."

They did and they did. Binding one end of the very red rope to the leg of a heavy wooden table, she threw the rest of the rope out of the window in the city wall—also the window of her apartment.

"Now get going before one of them spear chuckers comes back for tea or more."

"Thank you so much. How can we ever repay you?"

"You can't afford me, but promise me something."

"Anything," said the main spy without even a hint of hesitancy.

"When you and your soldiers come back to take Jericho apart . . . "

"Yeah."

"Promise me you will spare my family and me and my two cats, Sodom and Gomorrah."

"Lady," he said confidently, looking her right in the eyes, "we'll even spare your orange tree there in the corner."

"It's a lemon."

"Well, put some fertilizer on it. Don't give up on it so easy."

Post scriptum. Rahab's family was spared, although Sodom was lost in the shuffle of battle. All Rahab had to do was keep the same red rope hanging in her window and make sure that her parents and all the rest of her family were in her house when Joshua and his army returned and raised their horns to toot a tuneful oblivion. They blew Jericho away.

Much later than all that, in fact several generations down the line of Rahab's family tree—through her son Boaz—and on through the great king David, a name was added to Rahab's tree. Jesus.

So, Rahab's family tree was not a lemon after all.

JESUS SAID THAT WHEN SOMEONE HURTS US we should "turn the other cheek." Most of us wish it was the other guy's cheek.

• •

EVERY FAITH HAS ITS RITUALS and traditions. The Jewish tradition has Passover, Catholics have the Eucharist, Protestants have communion, Baptists have potluck suppers, and Episcopalians have happy hour. Our rituals and traditions are important as they remind us of who we are and where we've come from.

Lately, though, a lot of newer churches are dropping many of the old rituals. Some say the old rituals are empty and meaningless.

Many traditions of our faith are empty if we don't teach their meaning to young people. Without these rituals, younger believers will not know where their faith has come from; that is, handed down through the centuries. They will have "lost their spiritual address" as my friend Tony Campolo puts it. The sad part, I say, is that the family of God has been responsible for taking that spiritual address away from them.

Tradition is suggestion, not law. Sometimes it's a very good suggestion.

RIVER

A LOT OF STUFF IN THE BIBLE happens in, near, or through rivers. In fact, if you include lakes, oceans, and wells, well then, we'd have to say that water is a pretty important part of the Bible. (And leave us not forget rain and flood.)

One of the most interesting "rivermen" in the Bible—other than John (*See* John.)—was Naaman (pronounced Nay' mun).

Naaman was very, very rich. He was also very, very sick. You could actually see the sores all over his body. (See photo.)

In the midst of all his coughing and groaning, Naaman got a message from God. It was delivered by the neighborhood prophet. In the message, God told Naaman that the only way he could get rid of his sickness was to go down to the River Jordan and get completely underwater.

Sounds easy enough, but Naaman knew that the Jordan was a dirty, cruddy, yucky old river, so he asked God if he could merely sprinkle a little Jordan water on the top of his head. "Kind of a symbolic washing," Naaman insisted. "It's the thought that counts, right?"

God suggested that if Naaman wanted to get completely well, he would have to get completely wet.

"In fact," God was thinking on his feet, "why don't you go down seven times!" (You see, seven was God's lucky number.)

After a lot of discussion back and forth, Naaman went down for the seven count.

And it worked! When Naaman came up from his seventh time, every one of his ugly old sores had completely vanished. (*See* Vanished.)

Now, even though this story has been around for a long time and a lot of people have heard it, some people still don't want to try God's way of doing things: completely.

ROCK STAR

"THIS NEXT SONG ISN'T VERY SPECIAL to me: the Lord didn't write it and the words are kinda shallow and meaningless, but it's got a great beat that's almost as good as the Springsteen song it's copied after. Dig? Dig."

A SACRED COW

IN INDIA THE MOST POPULAR RELIGION believes that when you die, your spirit returns in another body. Which body you get—human or animal—depends on how you behaved in the first body. If you have been very, very good, you will come back as a cow. So in India, they do not kill or eat cows. In fact, they don't do anything to cows. They are allowed to wander around town, any town, as they please. What if the cow is an old neighbor or your dead Aunt Sarni? Even if you didn't like your aunt when she was just your aunt, it would not be polite to eat her now that she is a cow.

That's silly. If your aunt was good enough to come back as a cow, why wouldn't they let her live in the country on a quiet hillside? Why would they send a good old cow like Aunt Sarni back to her noisy, old neighborhood in the city?

These animals are called "sacred cows."

Everyone has stuff that's important to them, more important than anything else. It may be their job, their family, their church, their new SUV (Safer Under-All-Circumstances Vehicle), their gun collection, or an autographed picture of the president. They may be a person with an affable personality and a great sense of humor. They may even be able to joke about their bald spot or their big nose, but on this one subject (see list above) there shall be no humor. You shall not mess with my gun collection or picture of the president. We have our sacred cows, too. Besides, it would be silly to eat a picture of the president.

Self Image

MY SELF IMAGE would be fine if there weren't so many other people around to compare myself to.

A SERMON IS WHAT MOST PREACHERS DO EVERY SUNDAY morning in church. In some churches and synagogues, it is called a lesson and may occur on a Saturday evening. Baptists and a few others do it on Sunday nights when the dress code is usually a notch more relaxed. Some church folk give a sermon every time they open their mouths.

If the only way that people know about your faith is by what you tell them, maybe only your lips are religious.

All a sermon is, really, is "words about the words." It is somebody telling somebody else what something means. Very often that "something" is the words of Jesus put into our own words. More likely, these days, it is the words of the Apostle Paul explaining the words of Jesus. Even when

Jesus said something fairly simple like "Love your neighbor," there were people who didn't understand. Many chose to misunderstand. Paul chose to explain.

Jesus spent a lot of time explaining his words to the people who were closest to him and should have understood best.

Come to think of it, if the people that Jesus and Paul hung out with had been a little quicker on the uptake, the Bible, especially the New Testament, would be much shorter.

Much!

A sermon can also be seen in someone's life. Just watching the way a follower of Christ treats people can be a lesson about God. It really is true that Truth is often more powerful when it is caught than when it is taught.

A good sermon should be seen and not heard.

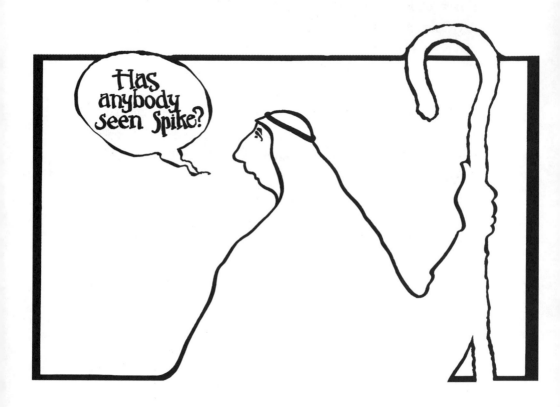

SHepherd

THERE ONCE WAS A SHEPHERD who had one hundred sheep. One cold night the shepherd noticed that one of his sheep was missing. (He always counted them, every sheep, every night.) He left his whole flock to go find the one little missing sheep. It wasn't the best sheep or the biggest sheep, it was just the missingest sheep.

Just like socks in the dryer, you can start with one hundred of them and when one is missing it becomes the most important thing in your life. Not because it's better, just because it's missing.

The shepherd did not come back until he found the missing sheep. When the shepherd found the little lamb he said, "The old flock just ain't the same without ewe."

You might say that God is your shepherd and Jesus is God come to find you, because to God, there's nothing more important than you.

SINGLES | Christians Seeking Christians

ONE OF THE BUSIEST SUBGROUPS in many churches is the singles group. These are churchgoers who are no longer in college, are not yet married, and do not have children. (If you are single and have kids, you go to the "Single-People-with-Kids-That-We-Don't-Have-a-Group-for" class.) One church went so far as to name their singles group the "Inbetweeners" because they were in between college and . . . the rest of their life.

I thought they were in between an hourly wage and a salary, or in between an apartment and a condo, or in between a Volkswagen Bug (the old kind) and a BMW.

Singles groups are comprised of interesting, gifted, talented, odd, vivacious, sometimes lonely, and often remarkable people. Not all of them are looking for a mate. Most would settle for someone to join them at Sizzler for lunch after church. LTR. Call 1452.

What follows is a small sampling of church singles from around the land.

SNAKE

THE STORY GOES that a snake handed a lady some fruit, and the next thing you know she was in a whole lot of trouble. Ever since then, snakes have not had hands or been allowed to talk.

ENTER THE MYSTERIOUS and distant land of Canaan. A group was sent ahead to assess the situation. So as not to be detected as outsiders or spies, they wore disguises.

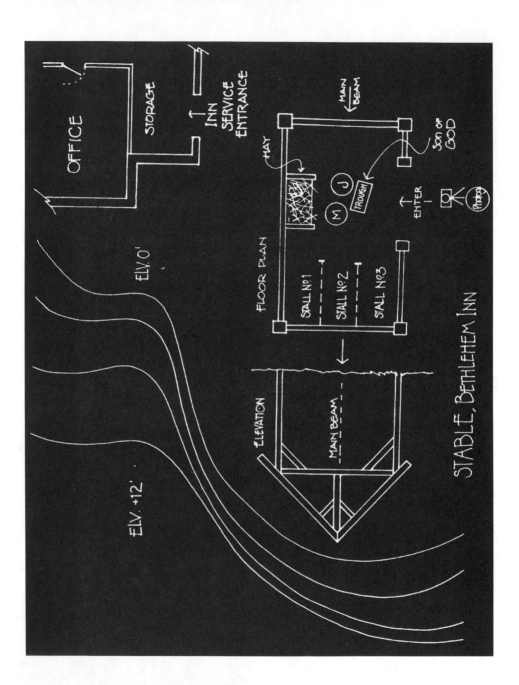

OFFICE

STORAGE

INN
SERVICE
ENTRANCE

ELV. 0'

ELV. +12'

FLOOR PLAN

HAY

MAIN
BEAM

Son of
God

M

J

TROUGH

ENTER

Photog

STALL Nº1

STALL Nº2

STALL Nº3

ELEVATION

MAIN BEAM

STABLE, BETHLEHEM INN

Stable

IT COULD WELL BE SAID that Jesus had a stable beginning.

TEN COMMANDMENTS

SOME PEOPLE DON'T LIKE THE TEN COMMANDMENTS, but for a movie that was made in 1956, you'll have to admit it was very impressive.

In one of the big scenes, Moses (played by Charleton Heston with a lot of white hair and a very interested look on his face, *See* Moses) goes up a big mountain to see God.

What Moses finds is a bush that is burning but doesn't get burned up! That would put an interesting look on anybody's face.

The bush also talks. Really, it's God's voice. Well actually, it's Charleton Heston's voice. (Orson Wells turned down the chance to be the voice of God.) Maybe that's how God really sounds to some people—just like your own voice. Who's going to remember what the voice sounded like?

It's what the voice said that's important.

That was about three thousand years ago. Today we have thousands of laws to help us remember what the voice told Moses, but they all boil down to two things: love God and don't hurt anybody.

THOMAS

IF HE WERE ALIVE TODAY, Thomas would live in Missouri. His favorite phrases were, "Oh, yeah?" and "Really?" and "You're kiddin' me?" and "Get outta here!" and "Prove it."

Some folks will believe almost anything they hear. Not Thomas. That's how he came to be known as Doubting Thomas.

He always wanted a second opinion. He wanted to hear it from the most reliable source. Thomas also said, "Seeing is believing."

When Thomas finally saw Jesus—after the resurrection—Jesus said, "Not seeing, yet still believing—that's believing!"

￼RADITION

IT JUST WOULDN'T BE the Sunday school convention without it!

This year it may have to be. Every year since he was eight years old, George Whippleman has kicked off the annual tri-cities nondenominational church confab with his rousing rendition of Rudy Atwood's stirring piano arrangement of "Sound the Battle Cry."

George Whippleman plays the accordion. But according to George, he will not start the annual three-day event this year with what has become "our national anthem" to most long-time attendees. No, this year George will not be playing "Sound the Battle Cry" on the opening day. Nor will he play anything else. He will not squeeze a single note from his Meltoner Deluxe with the mother of pearl buttons and real ivory keys. George is not sick. He is not going to be out of town on business; he has always been able to adjust his travel schedule as regional field demonstrator for the Melody Magic Music Co., "Makers of the world's finest accordions and mouth organs." George is healthy and very much in town. He is tired of playing "Sound the Battle Cry" and won't play it at this or any other event, ever. He refused to do it. This was his final answer. "And no one is going to make me feel guilty about it, either," said George.

Even George's Uncle Lionel (on his mother's side), whose sister Eileen had given George his first accordion lessons, could not persuade him.

166

Possibly worse than George's outright refusal to play was the problem of a replacement for the Sunday school convention. After all these years (George was now forty-one), no other accordion player in the state had ever even considered learning the piece. "George'll do it," they thought. "That's his piece. He'll do it until he dies." They were right; he'd been doing it for twenty-three years.

Not this year. Not anymore.

The program committee for the event even went so far as to contact Rudy Atwood himself. But Mr. Atwood was already booked to play GLASS, the Greater Los Angeles Sunday School convention. In desperation, an ad was placed in the Gospel Accordion Society's monthly bulletin (a.k.a. *GAS News*.) An eleven-year-old girl in Eufala, Alabama, wrote to say that she could play "Battle Hymn of the Republic" or the theme to *Battlestar Gallactica*. The music instructor from the Fundamental Gospel Academy in Grumblers Notch, Tennessee, sent along a video of her Gospeltones accordion choir playing "Lady of Spain." "We do the gospel version," the note with the video read. "We usually distribute printed copies of the lyrics to all our audiences."

There's a gospel version of "Lady of Spain"? The lyrics began: "Jesus the Christ we adore thee." The Tri-Cities Sunday School Association Program and Refreshments Committee voted 6 to 2 not to open this year's convention with thirty-seven junior highers playing "Lady of Spain" on thirty-seven accordions. The two votes in favor of inviting the Gospeltones thought "Lady of Spain" might fit nicely with this year's theme, Great Women of the Bible.

Along the way there were many a heated discussion about the same old song, but rendered on a different instrument, any instrument. Someone suggested a choir of pianos played by ministers of music from many different denominations. "I can see it now, ten, twenty, no fifty pianos all playing together, representing the chorus of believers and the harmony of different doctrines coming together to . . . "

"To do battle?"

"It would take a year to tune fifty pianos together!"

"No, it wouldn't. Some guy in Minneapolis did it back in the 1940s at a big youth rally. I read about it. Wilson was his name. He could help us pull it off."

"No. If it can't be George, we are not going to have 'Sound the Battle Cry' played on any other instrument by any other musician. Why, it'd be like reading the Creation account in Genesis chapter one, not from the King James version of the Bible, but from the Sears catalogue."

In the end they invited the lower-grades choir from First Academy, right here in town, to sing a selection of Fanny Crosby hymns. At the opening-day service the new president of the Sunday school association announced, "This year's gathering, 'Great Women of the Bible', is dedicated to George Whippleman."

A more fitting tribute could not be made to anyone.

A WORD OR TWO ABOUT THE BELOVED ACCORDION

CONSIDER THE ACCORDION, such a godly device. What then, do tell, is the official instrument of Hell? The honking car horn?

"Every time a bell rings, an angel gets their wings." Ergo, every time a car alarm sounds in the middle of the night, a devil gets their horns.

FOR GOD, there is no "if" in the word "unconditional."

UNDER NEW MANAGEMENT

SOMETIMES PEOPLE who own bicycle shops or gas stations decide to move to another town and open a drive-thru laser eye surgery shop. Before they move, they sell their store to a new owner. The new people paint the front of the building and put a sign in the window that says, "Under New Management."

The store still sells bicycles or gasoline, but the new owners always make improvements. Same store only better.

When people become Christians by choosing to follow the teachings of Jesus, they are the same person, the same personality, but with a few changes—for the better.

Now they are "under new management."

VANISH

VANISH IS THE PLACE where our sins go when we give them to God.

:Verse

WHERE THE WORDS LIVE. It is their address-chapter and verse. It is a way of finding your favorite sets of words. A way, too, of separating your most favorite set of words from the words around them that might tell you what they're really about.

3:16

Wine

"YES, THE MIRASSOU Petit Sirah will be just fine."

WISEMAN

WISEMEN WERE KINGS from the East (Southern Arabia and Persia, not Cleveland). A bunch of them came to see the newest and best king ever—Jesus.

It took them a long, long time to get to Jesus' house. They found his house by following a great light in the sky. They followed this light—perhaps a very bright star—for more than a year.

Most people think that there were only three wisemen. There were actually 14 wiseman, also at least 87 to 173 servants, cooks, camels, and camel wranglers, probably. We just say that there were only three so they will fit neatly on our coffee tables and mantels at Christmas.

(File: X)

ABOUT THE ONLY TIME of year we hear about "X" anymore is at Xmas time. That's when the whole world celebrates the birth of the baby "X." What really happened was, there was this Greek delicatessen (in Knoxville, Tennessee) that was having a big Christmas party. They wanted to invite the whole neighborhood. The owner,

Takis, decided to make a big "Christmas Party" sign and place it in the window of the downtown deli.

As it happened, they had only one window and it was fairly small for a storefront. They knew, though, that in their native Greek language the symbol for the name of Christ is "X."

So they made a sign big enough to fill the entire window that said, "Xmas Party." Not only did it fit in the small window of their deli, but the sign was also catchy.

Soon, Xmas signs began to appear everywhere—even though a lot of shopkeepers were unaware that "X" meant "Christ." These days a lot of folks prefer Xmas because they think using the "X" crosses out Christ.

Many Xians (followers of X) got very upset with all the Xmas signs. Some set up committees and had meetings and printed up flyers at the 24-hour copy shop and made T-shirts all protesting: "Keep Christ in Christmas."

But he was. Always had been and always will be. You can't X him out.

YHWH

YHWH IS NOT A RADIO STATION IN MINNEAPOLIS. It is the name of God.

God also answers to names such as "friend," "king," "comforter," "father," "Lord," and most often, "Help!"

* Long ago, the Jews believed that the name of God should not be said aloud, so they wrote it in a way that could not be spoken. Later, YHWH became "Jehovah" and eventually "Lord."

YOU ARE MUCH TALLER THAN I'D HOPED
You're much shorter than I had planned.
H&R. Zacchaeus
Roman Tax Code
HOW
MAKE
CHAIRS

ZACCHAEUS

A SHORT STORY

Jesus: Can we go some place and talk?

Zacch: Your place or mine?

Jesus: Better be yours. I don't have a place.

Zacch: What do you like to drink?

Jesus: Do you have any Constant Comment?

Zacch: So I'm told.

    (Pause)

    What's it like being the Son of God?

Jesus: What's it like being short?

Zacch: (Pause)

SOMEONE WHO IS VERY EXCITED about a cause, an idea, or a belief is a zealot. They have zeal—enthusiasm. Zealots are really "into it." If you've read this far in this book you are a zealot. You are into it.

About the Author

C. McNair Wilson has worked as a classroom teacher, film critic, summer camp staffer, graphic designer, cartoonist, actor, director, playwright, screenwriter, set designer, percussionist, ventriloquist, Sunday School teacher, magician, puppeteer, theme park designer, conference speaker, and ice cream shop manager. His creativity workshops for corporations—through his company Imaginuity Unlimited—includes clients as diverse as Apple Computer, Salvation Army, Sony, Bess Eaton Doughnuts, American College of Mortgage Attorneys, Universal Studios Florida, and the United States Government. During ten years with Disney, he was a concept designer at Imagineering for theme parks and resorts. He taught creativity throughout the thirty plus Disney divisions. He is a regular contributor to *The Door* magazine. McNair has performed his two popular one-man plays (*The Fifth Gospel* and *From Up Here*) over 1,500 times, everywhere. He is currently consulting on entertainment projects in four cities and working on three more books, for now. And then after lunch . . . He writes with fountain pen or on his Mac. He lives in the United Airlines baggage claim area of a major Bay Area airport.

About the Illustrator

McNair has collaborated with this author for years. His cartoons have appeared in publications from *Rolling Stone*, to *Leadership Journal, The (Wittenburg) Door Magazine,* and *Pasadena Star News.* He has illustrated books for other authors and turned down invitations to illustrate books he disagreed with philosophically. As a graphic designer (now semiretired), McNair's clients have included: John Denver Media, Youth for Christ, Minneapolis Children's Theatre, Walt Disney Co., CITA (Christians In Theatre Arts), and T.G.I. Friday's. Some of McNair's favorite drawings have been drawn for Chez Panisse Café (Berkeley), Mi Piace (Pasadena), Bouchon (Yountville), and House Restaurant (San Francisco) on their butcher paper and place mats. He prefers Tombo brush pens, Pentel Sign pens, Zig scroll and brush, and the ever faithful Sharpie. He has tried every pen on the market, twice, and he is a Macintosh-only person. McNair is available for dinner most nights of the week.

About the Press

PageMill Press publishes books in the field of spiritual growth. Its authors explore the emotional, psychological, social, physical, and practical dimensions of our daily lives from a spiritual perspective. The Press is committed to producing accessible and readable books for thoughtful seekers along a broad spectrum of issues within the Christian tradition.

The Press seeks to honor the writer's craft by nurturing the interior impulse to create, and thereby publishing books that encourage a reader's spiritual development and formation. PageMill Press regards highly the collaboration of publisher, editor, and author, and the creative expression of ideas, knowledge, and wisdom that results for readers.

Great care is taken to create beautiful books that improve the quality of our lives and which also can be given as gifts.

For a catalogue of publications of PageMill Press, for editorial submissions, or for queries to the author, please direct correspondence to:

PageMill Press
2716 Ninth Street
Berkeley, CA 94710
Ph. 510-848-3600
Fax. 510-848-1326

Notes & Doodles

Notes & Doodles

Notes & Doodles

Notes & Doodles

Notes & Doodles

Notes & Doodles

Notes & Doodles

Notes & Doodles